3 - 25 - 04

THE FALL
OF
TROY

THE FALL
OF
TROY

Imad Shouery

To order additional copies of this book, contact:
Xlibris Corporation
1-888-7-XLIBRIS
www.Xlibris.com
Orders@Xlibris.com
17859

CONTENTS

PREFACE

Familiar readers of the Iliad will notice that I have made some changes from the original work of Homer, especially with regard to Helen.

Herodotus made the claim that Helen was never in Troy during or before the war, but rather after sailing from Argos with Paris, they encountered a storm which enforced them to anchor in Egypt.

Herodotus also claimed, that Homer was well aware of this event, but he did not include this fact because it does not go well with the epic.

I have used Herodotus's version because it serves the theme of this poem, which is constructed about the arrogant misuse of power and the absurdity of wars.

I should also mention, that while the images and the major structure are constructed from the Iliad, the composition of the narrative in the dialogues is mine.

I.S.

ACKNOWLEDGMENT

I wish to express my deepest appreciation to my friend and colleague, professor Walter Bass for his constructive suggestions, and assistance in shaping this poem, and to my friends, Donald Jennermann, director of the Honor program, and chairman of the Humanity department, to Pat Dolan lecturer in the Humanities (both of Indiana State university) for their continuous encouragement and support.

I.S.

THE DEATH OF HECTOR

The setting sun of Ilium,
With a ring of dusty clouds,
Shadows the stillness of the wind,
Over the skyline of a dying kingdom.

And the silvery branches,
Of the olive grove,
In mourning wilted their velvety leaves.
When Hector lost his will to win,
Against Achilles' sharpest spear.

The Trojan soil was weeping,
From the scent of his musky blood,
With Achilles in trance and frenzy,
Euphoric with his rival's fall.

His passion steered by vengeance,
Blinding his mind with follies,
Drifting away from his kythara,
The Muses, and the Dionysian wine.

As a thundering storm was ramming
His chariot against the Iliums,
Whirl winding Hector's shredded body,
Blasting the pounding wind
Of the desolate plain,
With ghostly threats and cries.

For you, beloved Patroklos . . .
I spear; deeper I spear,
The corpse of Hector,
Impaling him down,
Cold to the ground,
Smearing with shame
The lions of Ilium,
This is the cure
To wash my grief,
And to enthrone
Your princely pride.

DOOMSDAY

While Achilles roamed
The battle field in frenzy,
Swollen with hubris
In heart, in veins.

The Argives were culling
The smoldering field,
Thrashing the ashes
For gold and silver,
As crown to their greed,
As signs of glory.

The Trojan flank succumbs to fear,
Their spears outnumbered,
Their shields defenseless;
These saviors of Troy
Are only children.
Waiting their fate,
To live or die.

The darkening clouds of doom,
Like a spiral wind,
Spinning a hopeless fate
Without direction
Foreshadow the face of Ilium
With mourning veils,
Before caving from time.

And the women of Troy,
Despite the quakes like thunder,
Circle the heavenly wall,
Like wreaths of wilting flowers,
And dance for Hector
His wedding dance
Singing and wailing,
Songs of lamentation,
In obeisance to departed hero,
To his city, he died too young.

THE EULOGY

The misty air thins the clouds,
Over the sailing sun of Ilium,
Drizzling the scent
Of the mountain's thyme
Over the stenchy horror
Of the battle field.

The marble of the Dionysian shrine
Melts, like candles burning
For a long day of mourning;
And the black bird
With its cry of death,
Pokes the wounds
Of decaying corpses,
As if the wings of fate,
Darken the face of Ilium.

Under the stoa
Of Apollo's shrine
Priam took his loneliest,
Loftiest stand,
With an aura shaped and woven
With silky flare,

Gathering his strength,
Mastering his will,
Squeezing the strings
Of his aging heart,
His voice bursting,
Like an Aeolian trumpet,
Lamenting the darkening days
Of the Trojan sky.

Oh me . . . Ilium,
A towering kingdom
In the foothill
Of the Anatolian mountains,
Mother of cities
In honor and deeds,
A blossoming dawn
Of justice and peace;
Your days are gone,
For ever gone.

A wretched, weak servant
I have been,
Failing to master the tide
Of the battle field,

Failing to guard your women,
Your children,
Your walls sky high,
Engraved with pride.

The weakness of my will,
Against your stubborn foe,
Has brought destruction,
And morbid agony.

Oh me . . . Ilium,
A curse has fallen upon you,
From heavenly hands,
Bringing destruction
With blazing fire,
From a stubborn foe.
The veins of my heart,
Are drying of life,
The dreams of my soul,
Succumbing to fear.
A heavenly hand only can save
Your fatherless children,
And change the murky days
Of your flight.

Oh me . . . Ilium,
If I have seeded wishful,
Or thorny dreams in your plains,
If I have blemished
Your deeds or covenant,
With greed or envy,
Let the sharpest spear of
Justice slay me cold,
For no righteous king,
Should ever stand above the law.

THE PRAYER

Oh Zeus, king of kings,
Father of all the gods.
No existing mortal or immortal,
Can share your wisdom and wit,
Power and glory.
Your throne is carved
With hands from heaven,
With perfect form,
In splendor and beauty.

No living man,
Nor yet to be alive,
Can fully grasp
The course of your design;
For kings and servants,
Masters and slaves,
You are the living mystery
Of heavenly laws;
From the mirror
Of your luminous conscience,
We yearn to draw
Our judgement and deeds,
To shape the laws
Of an earthly kingdom,
In the likeness
Of your shrine.

From the seat
Of your holy mountain,
In blissful mood
You contemplate the truth,
Observing heavenly laws
Governing the sphere.

Oh Zeus,
These days are my bleakest days,
Your presence I need.
To throw a light of meaning
Upon this road,
Where justice is overruled
By a stained sword,
Where man's highest euphoria
Is in killing other men.

I ruled this earthly kingdom,
With your holiness in mind,
With firmness for justice,
As the golden mean for piety.

But frailty in man,
Most awesome to surpass
When passion glows,
Will strike the human heart,
And reason drift away,
In judging right from wrong.

Oh Zeus,
In these ill-fated days,
Your light I need
To shed upon my conscience
The norms of heaven's laws.
Distrusting my frailty
In reading your mind,
I beg you for guidance
Before this kingdom's fall.

I ruled this kingdom justly,
Honoring the heavenly laws.
Should I shade my conscience
With prudence to survive?
Or should I face my fate with honor,
        Without submission to my foe.

THE CONFESSION

Oh Zeus, King of kings,
Father of all the gods.
These days are my darkest days;
Your help I need,
Not asking you to change
The tide of victory,
Of the Achaean
Tidal wave of fire.
Our days are shrinking,
Our hopes are gone.
Since the sharpest spear
Of god-like Achilles,
Took the last breath of life,
From my son Hector,
Our doom was signaled,
Our fate was drawn.

What I'm asking of you my lord,
Is death with honor.
Like the old oak tree
Of the rocky mountain,

Falling with grace,
And roaring pride,
Against the storm,
I wish to fall;
For the last stand,

Facing one's fate
With stern resolve,
Is how a just ruler
Ought to stand,
Without succumbing to fear.

My son Alexandros,
Carrying the purest seed,
Of the Trojan line,
Nurtured with love
From Hecabe's heart and soul.
Well trained in honoring justice
From well wishing seers,
Shielding his homeland with valor,
For freedom to fight with pride.

His shoulders arched,
Like an Aeonian pillar;
Upright in deeds,

His face shines with glittering colors,
Like a newly born rainbow
From the silvery glare
Of the mountain,
And the sprouting sea.

Alexandros was born
With virtues seeded in his soul,
With dreams to be
A courageous guardian,
A prudent shepherd for his land.
Young and lean, with youthful heart
And flowering dreams,
He sets his sails to wander
On the Achaeans' shores.

Not knowing what the gods
Are planning for his fate,
In luring Helen,
Of the glowing smile
From the Spartan strait.
Daughter of Zeus and Leda,
Most heavenly breed,
Wife of God-like Menelaus,
Guardian of the sea,

Her beauty unsurpassed,
By any living maiden,
Nor by the Cypriot Goddess;
Our heavenly queen.
Gazing at Helen
Through the misty clouds,
Her silky frame,
Glowing with passion,
Her golden hair
Nested with stars,
His boyish heart
Was charged with lust,
To leap into
The Achaeans' hill,
To lure her swiftly
From her land.

Alexandros was schooled
With virtues and respect,
For heavenly laws,
But passion struck,
And blurred his vision,
And vanity blinded
All his mind.

A sly barbarian could not equal
His brute temper,
In besieging and dishonoring
Innocent spouse,
And force her quenching
His desire.
The sin of sins,
The meanest of all sins,
Has fallen with gloom
Upon this peaceful kingdom
A blunder from a fool
A senseless fool,
Bringing most shameful shame,
With blazing fire.

Oh me, a wretched, weakling king
Not fit to rule
If my heart swayed my will,
Not willing thus the law,
Against my kin or foe.
Ruthlessness for truth,
Is unwelcome course,
But a virtuous king
Should have the sense
To take a stand.

My feeble heart,
My powerless will,
The instinct of fatherhood
Betrayed my heavenly call.
Instead of choosing justice
Against Alexandros,
To live a homeless hound,
Unwillingly I have chosen,
        This kingdom's fall.

THE PLEA

Oh Zeus, King of kings,
Father of all the gods,
The darkest cloud has fallen upon
This peaceful kingdom,
Folding its fate,
Its glorious past, to the unknown.
Our fatherless children
Will be disposed into Hades,
Our women will be enslaved
By ruthless masters,
And those who were behind
The slaughtering line
Will become homeless,
Living off scraps
From neighboring lands.

What will be left of
The smoldering ashes?
Only echoes,
Of the unmerciful slaughter,
Hanging in thin air,
To find a place in time,

Waiting to be reseeded in memories
To tell its own untailored story
About man's futile craving
For greed, power, and glory.

Illusion, most incurable illusion,
Seeking power with merciless heart.
Destroying cities,
Dethroning kings, subduing foes.
Waging endless wars,
Will generate an endless doom.

Lacking the wisdom
To control barbaric passion,
Rulers often seek for glory
By waging wars.
After subduing by sword
The neighboring land,
Often they turn their wit
To new domain,
Not realizing that in trying
To enslave others
They unknowingly become slaves
Of their own craving.

Oh Zeus King of kings,
Father of all the gods.
As you can see from your throne,
Agamemnon's wrath will not fall short
Of sacking, destroying,
Putting ablaze the shrines of Troy,
For no defending shields
Can face his raging fire.

After the fall of Hector's shield,
All Trojan shields are doomed to fall.
My princely son, my beloved son,
Most courteous heart of the Trojan breed

Fighting a war not for his own,
But for the honor of his deeds,
Pinned to the ground
By the son of Peleus' spear.

What could be more dishonoring
For an aging man,
Than the living shame of his son's corpse
Sinfully exposed in open air
For straying dogs
And scavenging birds?

What an aching pain
For his wife's heart,
What smoldering hopes,
For his son's soul.
And Hecabe, a mother of mothers,
A divine grace,
Her limbs are trembling,
Her bones imbued with pain.
Tireless from waiting
For a sign from a falling star,
To deliver Hector's body
From the wrath of Achilles.
Incense she burned to wipe the spell
Of evil thought,
With myrrh and olive branches,
Adorning the arches
Of the western gate
To please the gods,
So they bring peace,
          And fresh new hopes.

THE APPEAL

Waiting and waiting for a sign
From a falling star,
Exasperated with his hopes,
Yet tenacious in mind and soul,
Priam took a lofty stand
Facing the altar
Towards the heaven,
Echoing his grief and pain
To father Zeus,
Lamenting his fallen son.

Like an aging eagle
Spreading his wings,
Before setting
For his lonely flight.
He spread his arms
With an outcry for mercy,
With tears dripping
From swollen eyes.

Oh Zeus, father of all the gods.
What a suffering pain,
What a morbid thought
Invades his mind.

In every moment I think
Of Hector's corpse
Exposed for mockery in open air.
Indignity and wretched feeling
Goads my heart.
What an impotent weakling king I am,
If I cannot master
My fate and wit,
To bring my son to Ilium,
For his burial rights,

If you my lord, most immortal of the gods,
Limit your judgement upon the dead
For torturous punishment or reward,
Then how can a mortal god-like Achilles
Extend his ravaging wrath
Against my son Hector
Beyond the limit of your domain?

If justice is succumbing to power,
My aging heart and brittle bone,
Calling upon my conscience to perform
A task beyond my power and domain,
Instead of dying slowly a thousand deaths,
I choose to die once
From a flying spear,
Appealing to Achilles my rightful cause,
To free my son Hector
In honor of the heavenly law.

PRIAM AND HECABE

My spouse, my beloved friend
In grief and joy,
You've always been
My counselor and companion,
A soothing comfort,
For my soul.
More than ever,
I need your wisdom and sober mind,
To face the darkest moment
Of this war.

Knowing too well
The lack of prudence in my plan,
You may rejoice,
Or sadden with my thought,
When I unravel the thread
Of my undue desire.
Sleepless with disquieting heart,
Consumed with grief,
I wait for news from Achilles,
Or a hopeful signal
From the Olympian gods,
To lift my soul.

While in my deep pondering
To ease my grief,
A vision throttled my mind
To make a move
To go shield less
With precious gifts to Achilles,
Appealing to his heart,
And reasoning for fairness,
To bring Hector to Ilium,
For his resting place.

Hecabe rejoiced
When she heard Priam's solemn words;
Addresses him
With assurance in her voice:

You have just spoken
What has been perking in my heart.
In these dark moments
Of agony and deep despair
No man could ever take
Your lonely stand,
With dignity you face this wrath
With peaceful soul,

Lofty in spirit,
With mind so well composed.
Patience could reach its limit,
When one faces a stubborn foe.
What else can you decide
Except pursuing your plan?
Asking Achilles for mercy

For Hector's sake
Will be serving a higher cause.
This should be done,
Not only for our courageous son,
But for what is divinely just
According to the heavenly laws.

My lord I only have a plea
For my own sake.
Since you will be pursuing
A perilous road,
Why don't you let me be
Your partner in this cause?
If you accept, an eternal joy
Will crown my life;

If you reject, towards this altar
I will stand,
Praying to the Olympian gods,
For your return.

Gazing at the brilliance
Of Hecabe's solemn face,
Priam was shrouded
By her wisdom and resolve.
With gestures stressed by his wavering voice,
He reaffirmed the divinity of their vow.

I do not doubt
Your readiness to sacrifice,
To give your heart and soul sincerely
With genuine care
But If destiny forbids
Your most earnest call,
Do not take it a feather shy
From my acclaim of you.
My spouse, my friend,
A comforting council in grief and joy.
Inside these shattered walls,
You will be needed most;
By divine right,
And my entrusted will,

As Queen you will be heading
This council justly.
During my absence,
Or if I am hunted down,
With your willing, I will convey
My thought and plan
To the council, to the guardians,
And to the seers.

PRIAM MEETS THE COUNCIL

At dawn break,
Priam met the council and the seers,
To show his plan
For ransoming Hector
From the unforgiving wrath
Of Achilles.

The young were stunningly surprised,
The old read well his mind with cheers.
Priam with his collected mind,
Took his stand with firm resolve,
Fearless, poised, and serene.

Most trusted citizens of the land,
Enshrined with virtues,
Guardians of the law,
For ten days past anxiously waiting,
Hector's body is not home.
Strangulated with guilt and shame,
His corpse engraved
Upon my conscience,
A moral claim.

Morbid fixations invade my thought,
Haunting me with agonizing dreams.
No courageous king
Would seek mercy from his foe,
But for a humble, rightful cause
I chose to risk
My life and honor,
To ransom Hector's mutilated corpse.

What I am asking of you is clear;
With Aeneas gone, Hector gone,
Alexandros unfit to rule,
If Achilles extends his wrath,
And slays me cold,
A loyal course
I ask of you for Hecabe,
Mother of mothers,
As sister, and as a queen.

A wave of silence swept the air;
The councilmen and the noble seers,
Rose from their seats
Like pointed spears,
In rhythmic wave were chanting,
Their voices piercing the wind,

Eulogizing Hector in singing dirges,
In disheartened mood shedding their tears.

Oh lord, our king and servant,
Our hearts and souls
Will shade your journey
With contemplative prayers,
Incense will be burning
For your honor and safety
In tending your noble cause.
And for Hecabe
Our benevolent queen,
Nothing less than loyalty
We offer her in this house,
An eternal flame for justice,
In wars and prosperous peace.

THE JOURNEY

Priam called upon Idaeus,
The oldest of the mules' breakers,
And the wisest driver of the team.
He reads well the right passage;
Swiftly keen in avoiding danger
Under tension, with resilience,
He can steer.

A long day ahead is waiting,
Before we set the mules
Towards the reef
Where the black ship of Achilles is anchored,
Sheltered from the northern wind,
And protected from our spear.

Sharp eyed Idaeus; noble in character,
And well refined in breed.
When the dust is settled,
From the clashing horses,
And the air is cooled
From flying spears,
We should be heading
Towards the Argives' camp.

To take the ransom for Hector's body
To the slayer of men, Achilles.

A long day of work is waiting,
To clean and brush a strong
But graceful pair of mules.
To wax and shine
The most ornate gears.
Prepare Dionysus' sacred carriage
Which I ride to welcome his rebirth
When life from the pores
Of mother earth appears.

Like a soft misty breeze
Before the setting of the day,
Priam made his move
Towards Hecabe's maiden room,
To fetch her thought
For what may please
Achilles' senses and desires.

They both descend into
The sacred treasure chamber;
Their eyes were fixed
Upon their cedar wedding chest,
A present from a Sidonian prince.

With the speed of a diving hawk
Upon its victim,
They filled it with enchanting gifts
In craftsmanship,
Rich in substance, and in form
The silver cups engraved
With gold for sacrament,
The crystal lamp
With mother of pearl edging its rim,

Gleaming in darkness
Like a rainbow in the spring;
Garments woven with virgin silk
From Anatolia,
Pregnated with glowing colors
Of Tyrian dye.
Laces and gems, fragrances and spices
From the east,
To bring allurements
To Achilles' heart and desires.

Before the rosy clouds
Glazed all the Trojan sky,
Idaeus was swiftly yoking
His graceful mules.
The carriage was polished
With olive oil and brine.
The drums were greased,
The spikes were shined
With bee wax, cedar resin
And frankincense,
Ready to glide smoothly,
To the Argives rocky line.

As Idaeus swiftly drove
To the chamber door,
Lordly Priam was ready
For his long journey,
With peaceful mind and soul,
Resolved to the unknown.

When Priam signaled
To mount the sacred wagon,
Idaeus was eagerly ready to steer.
Unwillingly Hecabe began to shed
Her crystalled tears.

May Zeus, father of all the gods,
Be with you lord,
And the steel hearted Athena
Soften her verdict,
To bring you back
Safely with Hector,
To lament him, singing dirges,
With the outcry of our lyre.
And Cassandra wailing,
With her mandeely waving
O lord of heaven, help my father
To pursue his rightful cause,
For his deeds are the same deeds
Engraved in heaven.

After they mounted
The four wheeled wagon,
Yoked with the strongest
And most graceful mules,
Priam took the right side seat
Of noble Idaeus,
As if he is co-piloting
The mules towards the plains,
Commonly dressed
With a heel length garment,

As if he was a herald
Of a Theban priest.

And Idaeus, wearing
Stoic attire,
Sharply directed at the mules
His piercing eyes,
Lest they sniff unwelcome danger
From the wind,
Swiftly he sets his course
Towards god-like Achilles.

With humble tone in voice,
And graceful gesture,
Priam asked good hearted
And noble Idaeus,
What course should we pursue
On this risky journey
To reach safely the hut
Of god-like Achilles?
Idaeus frowned while focussing
His stern attention,
But soon he caught his senses
With a noble smile.

My lord, since you have made your plan;
Sleepless I've been,
Praying to Zeus,
Father of the Olympian gods.
But then a light darted
Into my sleepless mind,

Furrowing a path
Through the Myrmidonian line.
The reason for this flashing light
I do not know,
But my heart tells me,
It's the safest to follow.

Attentive in mood,
Priam frisked his beard,
Humbly bowed his head,
Gesturing in repose,

There is good reason
For your sight, noble Idaeus.
The Achaeans are short tempered,
And quick in action,
Which is a frailty
On which reason may glow.

The Myrmidonian do not have
Big stakes in this war;
After they soothed their vengeance
For Patroklos' loss
They might be good listeners
For our just cause.

Idaeus jerked the lash,
And the mules smoothly moved
The four wheel wagon
Towards the Myrmidonian line
As if destiny bestowed

On Priam his finest moment,
With a vision of a life time
As prince for peace,
Facing a world infested
With greed and lust for glory.

The dusk was spreading
Its velvety shroud,
Over the olive groves
And the misty meadows.
The swallows were sweeping
The emptiness of space

To spread good wishes
For Priam on his journey.
The mules steadfastly moving,
The sacred wagon
Rhythmically ground the wheels
Against the rocky path,
Its face dimly stained
With the horror of slaughter,
Its skyline dismembered
By the olive grove and pine.

Priam and Idaeus
Wandered in silence,
The anguish in their heart,
Like silent music,
Could not be translated
Into words or rhythms.
What a cynical craft,
Man has invented for slaughter.
Destroying peaceful cities,
And leveling holy shrines.

And all for naught,
Ages of labor and pain
To build a temple,
A place to dwell in peace
Under the divine laws,
Because of a moment
Of blind passion,
All could fall and crumble,
In seeking senseless power
        And craving for glory.

THE ENCOUNTER

While Priam and Idaeus
Gazed at the battle field,
Stared at decaying horses,
And others still struggling to die
Beheaded corpses with gushing parts,
With killing stench cluttering the sky,
Armors corroded, and gears broken,
Shields dented with hammering clubs,
And drilled with deadly spears.

From every corner and every sight,
Deafening silence, unfolds a story
Of men unleashing their passion with hatred
To slake their thirst for fame and glory.

The mules were still pulling
The wagon smoothly,
Then suddenly halted
With a frantic move
Loudly began to bray,
As if danger
Or a visitor were standing by.

Promptly Idaeus swayed
His mules from what they feared,
Clutching the brakes
That he might stop,
To give his pair
Affirming touches with his hands.

The twilight was fading
Into a moonless night,
When a Myrmidonian guard
Suddenly appeared.

I am Argeiphontes,
A Myrmidonian guardsman
From the flank of Achilles,
A god-like warrior,
Like thunder in wars
And most tender hearted in peace.

Who are you old stranger,
Drifting in this terrain?
Are you spies for Priam
Or feebly wandering,
Aimlessly probing
This dangerous land?

I am Priam of Troy . . .
And this is Idaeus,
Loyal friend and partner,
A noble man indeed.

We are on a risky trail
Seeking lordly Achilles,
To sooth my wounds and pain
From this ravaging war.

As you can see clearly,
Empty handed we are;
No vengeance do we proclaim,
Nor threat we have at heart;
We mounted this old wagon
Without our shields and spears,
By mules driven, not by horses,
For hauling, not for war.

Noble Argeiphontes,
I must confess to you
What is throbbing my heart,
With hope and will to live.

It is a wishful dream to shade
The end of my journey
By ransoming Hector's corpse
From lordly Achilles.

Our journey therefore,
Is not driven by chance,
Nor by any random
Prowling of our fate.

After long sleepless nights,
Anxiously counting days
Of sorrow, Hecabe's
Bones melted for her son.

With anguish in our hearts,
Incense and myrrh we burned,
Solemnly we performed
Our holy sacred rights.

Hoping the Olympian gods
Will sooth Achilles' heart,
Remove his wrath and vengeance
Against the son of Troy.

When grief consumed my soul,
And the darkening doom
Closed over the threshold
Of my final days.

A light sunk in my heart,
Uplifting me from death
With visionary dreams
To guide me on this path.

Noble Argeiphontes,
Here I am the king
Of a glorious kingdom
Where justice was glory.

At a whim of your sword,
You can behead me now,
Or if you have mercy
Make me your captive.

For if my fate brings light,
I can see Achilles,
And give him this ransom
For my son's shredded corpse.

I am only a guardsman,
My duty is the law,
In peaceful time a friend
You'll be, and not a foe.

I am perplexed my lord
Not sure what I should do;
A king of your stature,
Defeated, yet at peace.

Stepping into the unknown,
Leaving behind all fears,
Almost like immortals
With your mind and soul.

I am perplexed my lord,
My senses are confused.
The state of my conscience
Stands against what I must do.

But as a loyal guardsman
Fighting for Achilles,
Choosing what is right or wrong
Is not in my domain.

The laws of war, often
Lies in the strongest hand
Which can rend deadly blows
Faster than flying spears.

Within this zone the stranger
Is target for the bronze,
Without a plea for mercy
Or waiting for appeal.

I am facing a conflict,
Am torn between two laws.
Laws for peace, descending
From the norms of heaven,
And man-made laws for war,
For conquest and for glory.

King Priam, lord of Troy,
Is this a daring gamble,
A calculated risk,
Or a courageous gesture
Beyond what mortals do?

Shield less you come strolling
This dangerous road,
Content, peaceful and serene
Without the fear of death.

If I release my spear,
To pin you to the ground,
I will go on living
With dreadful guilt and shame
For not acting according
To my conscience-call.

For this reason alone
I'll lead you on your course,
Risking the wrath of Achilles,
A choice I have to take.
Because if man is human,
He must honor his choice.

Noble Argeiphontes
Bestowed with the divine,
Most righteous of mortals
Refined in wit and deeds.

Goodness is your substance,
Fineness is your form.
A gift not given by men,
Nor can be taken away.

In spite of all the follies
Of this ravaging war,
A mystery subdued
My soul with bliss and joy,
A price not high to pay
For meeting heart to heart.

Noble Argeiphontes,
Now take the lead,
Take me as captive
To lordly Achilles.

If the Olympian gods
Read well my wishing heart,
They will clear the air
From ills, and harmful thought.

My fate will be decided
When I meet Peleus' son
A welcome with mercy
Or impalement by his spear.

Graceful Argeiphontes
With gentle voice he spoke
His mind to lord Priam:

If friendship is born to last,
With blessing from the gods,
Then no one should take the lead,
Nor any shall follow.

With firm beliefs in justice,
We shall seek lord Achilles;
With a sign from the gods,
He might bestow his blessing;
Or if he is still in rage,
With a whip of his sword
We will fall without mercy.

With peaceful resignation,
They sighed in peaceful hymns.
Despairing of their fate,
They mounted for their journey.

The twilight was setting
Across the desolate plains
Its golden misty clouds,
The leaves of the poplar trees
Were motionless and pale
Over the embanking guards.

Suddenly Argeiphontes
Waved at Idaeus calmly
To slow the pace of his cart,
Before the Myrmidonian gate.

To leap unnoticed quietly
Into the quarter of Achilles
And brief him the news
Of his day-long journey,
And beg him for mercy,
      For Priam and his guide.

THE MEETING BETWEEN PRIAM AND ACHILLES

When Achilles heard the news
From Argeiphontes,
He was puzzled, perplexed,
Almost in disbelief,
For even Agamemnon
Would lack the courage,
To cross the line
Of the Myrmidonian gate,
But with Odysseus craftiness
And skill to cool the air,
He counseled Agamemnon
To dispatch his heralds
When he demanded
To have possession of Briseis.
But here is king Priam;
Unarmed he stands alone,
With his thin frame
As tall with pride as the sky is high.
With peaceful mind,
Fearless like the immortals,
As if he had cast already
His frightful fate away,

Without questioning his mind
For pain or joy,
In spirit high,
And heart to endure calamity.

If in defeat and agonies
Self contained,
He must be a god-like ruler
In peaceful time.
No wonder that the Trojans
Surround him with loyalty.

After he pondered with anguish
Upon his stand,
Hesitant, but gracefully
He moved to the gate,
And greeted Priam
According to the holy norms.

What kind of posture King Priam,
Are you taking?
Out of contempt you wish
To challenge my deeds,
Or did some god sway your will
With a heavenly call?

No mortal would dream
Of challenging your pursuit,
Unless he were guided
By an unknown god.
Not only your life
You are putting at stake,

With dishonorable death,
But you are also risking mine.
Agamemnon will be happy
Of your pursuit;
A mockery he will make
Of the Myrmidons,
And a ravaging war
Will split the Achaean camp.

Priam welcomed lord Achilles
In kneeling down,
His arms wide open
And his eyes facing the sky.

Oh father Zeus,
If I hold evil contempt
Toward god-like Achilles,
Strike me from heaven,

And reduce me to ashes
With your thunderbolt.
And you lord Achilles,
If you read well my mind,
And if you find vile
Or sinful signs within my soul,
Draw fast your sword,
Without regret behead me dawn.

I am here to beg you
For Hector only,
A leaf fallen before its time
From the Trojan sky.
He fought for his city
Against an honorable foe,

But with dishonor I live
Without his burial right.
My cause is simple;
To do what fathers do.
To give him burial
According to the law.

I do not blame you
For hating my son Hector,
Who slew your friend Patroklos
In front of the wall.

But my lord, your friend
Was given holy burial,
And my son's corpse remains
Exposed for straying dogs.

Regardless of the price,
Including my own life,
I beg you for his corpse
To give him a burial
According to our laws.

It is better to die,
Than live with shame.
My life is in your hand,
And the treasure of Troy;
Hecabe has filled
Her cedar wedding chest,
With what we have of ornament,
Tonic and wine;
I need a helping hand
Of your valiant doormen,
For we are too frail Idaeus and I
To hold it fast.

In a trance-like mood,
Engulfed with sadness and pain,
Achilles gave utterance
Like an oracle.

What brought you to my hut
Would have brought my father too,
Who was your equal
In dignity and pride.

Your visit has no price
With all the gleaming gold;
A ransom is not needed
To take your son Hector home.
I feel the pain of guilt
In prolonging vengeance.
With Hector's death
Hatred is out of place;
When passion strikes the heart,
It blinds the mind.
But does not justify,
Breaking the holy law.

I am grateful to know,
That an honorable foe,
Can be better then
A conniving partner;
If justice over-rules
Conflict among people,

There would be no reason
To master the plain,
Nor for building fleets,
To master the open sea
For a continuous state of wars,
And glories.

I joined this war believing
It is a rightful cause,
But Agamemnon has done no better
Than his foe
If Paris betrayed justice
For his own pleasures
In abducting Helen
Menelaus' maiden,
Agamemnon's action
Is no better against me.
If the abduction of Helen
Started this war,
Then how does he justify
Taking my Briseis?

Wars are made for show
Of force, for greed and glory,
Not for honor in defense
Of father land.
For this reason I am
Engrossed with guilt and shame,
For no good reason
All these men have lost their lives.
As my fate is written,
I too will forfeit mine.

Priam was elated
Hearing Achilles,
Display an overture
Of Delphic vision
Shepherd of the Myrmidons
God-like with his shield.
Enshrined with luminous wisdom
So young at heart,
As if he never waged a war,
Nor tossed a spear.

Priam was bewildered,
Ecstatic in his mood;
He felt inner peace,
Despite his broken heart;
He gathered his strength
To sharpen his mind and thought,
Weeping like a child,
But peaceful in repose.
With golden words,
Addressing lordly Achilles:

My lord this war has been
Tormenting me with grief.
I lost my sons except
Who caused this agony;
And most valiant Hector,
Still lying in your court,
Without his burial rights,
Prescribed by divine laws.

Meeting you and listening
To your golden words,
Assured me well
That Hector's death was not in vain,
He fought a god-like hero,
And lost to your spear.

In wars, those with honor
Will pay the price for all.
In vigilance, courage, and wit,
You have no equal;
I pray, asking the gods,
To save you from a sly.

What you have said
About the nature of wars,
Is clearly true,
Using the ugliest crafts
Invented by men,
Other than defending
Our land from intruders,
They are evil means
To justify killing,
And power and greed,
To rule a neighboring land.

But those with principles
Will bite their tragic fate,
Because for principles
They meet their tragic end.

And those who are like snakes,
Dwells in wavy trenches,
Survive the battle field
And become rulers,
Using power not to
Protect their subjects
From those who risk
Breaking the heavenly laws,
Or from barbarian onslaught
To kill and steal,
But to gratify their power
For power's sake,
Using it blindly
With arrogance and greed.

For this reason kings
Will become extinct as rulers;
They become traders of justice,
Ruling for trade.
If they refuse to rule,
Serving the trading cause,
Traders will become
Kings, makers of peace and war.

And war will become
A perpetual evil
Under the disguise
Of liberty and freedom,
But in fact a means
To enslave humankind.

Reflecting upon Priam's
Account and his views.
Achilles while listening
Was gazing in despair,
As if detached
From helmet and gear;
Suddenly he approached Priam,
Clasping his pointed cheek.

After this long journey
It is time for all to eat,
A maiden will arrange
Your bedding for comfort,
An attendant will clean
The gear and feed the mules;
Tonight we break our bread,
And share our food and wine,
And before the dawn break
        You'll go with Hector home.

THE FEAST

When the feast was ready
The maid signaled by call,
Achilles beckoned his guests
To share the wine
Idaeus took his seat
Across Argeiphontes,
And Priam sat across
Facing Lord Achilles.
With welcoming gesture
Achilles addressed his guests,
For king Priam's safety,
And good health for all.

Lets celebrate this friendship
In war and in peace
This gathering I am sure
Is blessed by all the gods,
For no other power
Could bring us heart to heart.

With solemn acknowledgment
Of these golden words,
Priam was inwardly gazing
To control his tears.
Then with stuttering voice
Addressed lord Achilles:

My solemn wish my Lord,
Is nothing short of peace,
We will accept the pain
Of hunger and disease.
The shattering despair
Of our hungry children,
The ravaging cold wind
From the northern hemisphere.
If this war can be ended,
With our silver and gold,
Agamemnon is free
To take all what we have
If he withdraw his siege,
And pledge his word for peace.

Achilles by now was,
In an amiable mood.
The crystal sparkling wine,
Had slowed his senses down,
With a friendly gesture,
He questioned the King of Troy.

If you desire peace
And willing to sacrifice
Then why not give us Helen,
The cause of this war?

Agamemnon will be
Obliged to sign the truce,
Because all his allies
Will not be bound to fight.

My lord, master of the battlefield,
I give you my word, and my honor,
And all the power bestowed upon me,
By my people and the gods,

Pledging your safety to go to Troy,
With all its doors opened
To your holiness
To see with your own eyes
If golden Helen, or Menelaus' treasure,
Are in between our walls.
In spite of my old age,
If I do not honor my words,
I deserve to be called a sly.

What all the maidens know or hear
About Helen's fate,
Is when Paris goes astray
With his gazing mood.
Mumbling her name with agonies.

At times, he mindlessly goes on
Wandering in the hallways,
As if he is consumed with pain,
Exhaling into the misty air,
Sigh, after sigh.
Calling her name,
As if he is in a trance
Recollecting names and words,
From foreign places,
Not familiar in our land.

As I recall when he returned
From his sinful journey,
He was alone strolling,
As if he is in deep despair
The gods may only know
What happens in his journey,
But I assure you,
That when he entered the gate,
Helen was not escorting him,
Nor any treasure carrier on his side.

The only tale is told
About his disastrous fate,
Is from a Phoenician trader,
Whose route is from Egypt to Tyros,
And from Tyros to Troy.

He claims that a Trojan prince
Drifted with a tidal wave
To the Egyptian shores.
After he was rescued
By the royal guards,
Suspicion was raised about
His rare and valuable belonging,
And his mistress
Of heavenly form.

King Proteus thought
That he might be a lone pirate,
A slave trader, or a master minded thief.
Who abducted a goddess like maiden,
From her land.

But before he unveiled his true identity
He paid tribute to the gods.
According to the Egyptians' norms,
He was set free by the royal court
To meet his own fate.

But golden Helen and her treasure
Were ordered to be guarded
At the royal palace,
Until she can return safely,
To her beloved homeland.

This is the truth
About what happens my lord.
Like I have giving you my word
To go safely to Troy.
I will extend my vow,
To lord Agamemnon
Or any of his counselors,
For peace might be restored,

Achilles was overwhelmed
By Priam's straight forward reply,
But puzzled and bewildered
About the state of this war.

If Helen is not in Troy,
Which I presume is true,
The gods should know
Where she must be.
Then what is their intention
For taking sides in this war?

Is it a titanic menace
Against the Argives and the Trojans,
To reduce them to ashes
For some unknowable sinful deed
They may have performed.

Or some kind of a baffling trickery
In using Helen as a ploy.
To see if we can use our reason rightly,
When the tide of passion,
Is in its uproar.

If I approach Agamemnon
To tell him the truth,
I am sure that he will not
Only challenge my words,
But he will try to mock me
For my stand.

Therefore, silence
Is sometime a virtue,
Because if my pride is tested again,
Dissension may take place
And a catastrophe may unfold.

What a useless senseless way
To solve a conflict,
What a blunder to fight a war
For a wrong cause,
Destroying cities
Displacing children
To meet their death,
Without knowing the reason
For their agonies.

What a wasteful way
To consume human passion
In using hatred,
As a means to divide and rule.

Instead of giving reason
A chance to ponder,
We become subdued
By our barbaric instinct
To sanctify our claims
By means of waging war.

A fruitless endeavor
Endlessly will go on,
Until an awakening
Enlightens man's soul
To realize that wars
Will not solve a problem,
But myriads of problems
Will generate from wars.

Achilles was speaking
As if he were in a trance,
Gazing at Priam
As if time were standing still.

Here a man
Whose favorite son I slew,
Whose son slew Patroklos,
The best of all my friends.

When we met heart to heart
Across the killing field,
It was as if a mystery
Transformed this bloody war,
Into a new covenant,
Where justice prevails for all.

After grasping his pride,
For doing what is right,
I have no reason to go on
Fighting this war
In spite of his old age,
His loss and weeping heart,
Peaceful, serene,
A god-like shroud upon his face,
Self-surpassing in resiliency and resolve.

Against this man in whose face
I see my father's face,
Who is more like a trusting friend
Than a mean foe.

In days I will be
Littering his land again,
With dismembered bodies,
Broken helmets and gear,
When I swiftly drive my chariot
To spear his men.

Lucky Hector I envy you
For your peaceful death,
Consciously you choose
To die for a good cause,
Splashing your blood
Against the wall of your city,
A choice you made
And rightfully fulfilled.
Your death, was a hero's death,
Fighting for your cause.

But if the prophecy is true
About my fate,
I will be facing my own death
Early in the spring,

Because I gave my word
To king Agamemnon,
Who in return betrayed
My honor with deceit.

I too, do not know
The craft of twisting words.
If I can take a stand
Against my own honor,

The ropes of the black ships
Will be cut off, and the sails
Will be gliding towards
My father's land.
But here I stand alone
With a choice for my doom.
It is better to meet

My death unhappily,
Than break a promise
And live with dishonor.

Priam gazed reflectively
Upon Achilles,
A god-like in stature,
With innocence at heart,
Like a living legend,
Near perfection he stands,
In form, and in substance,
With spirit to endure,
As if eternity
Has shaped him with its hand.

Time was sleeping
Between the real and the unreal,
And whims of silent gestures
Capturing his thought.

As if he was transformed
Into other worldliness,
Where grief, longing and joy
Elapse into ecstasy.

Priam was seized by sadness
And reflective thought,
Listening to Achilles'
Account of his life,
As if he were reciting
His own eulogy.

Knowing that his choice
Cannot alter his fate,
Without living in denial
Of his beliefs;
He accepted
His commitment to the war.

Priam began to stutter
His words like an oracle,
As if he were making prophecies
About wars.

The future of man
Is rooted in his dignity,
When dignity is lost
We all become enslaved.

Winners of wars, often
Ride their high passion,
Like swift eagles they think,
The sky is their domain.
Not knowing that a flea
Can pinch them deep in their nerves,
And cause enough pain
To change their hunting plan.

And those good hearted warriors
So often die in vain,
Misled by their rulers,
To fight an unjust war.
And used by them like bridges,
To widen their terrain.

As long as men are ruled
By their barbaric instinct,
War remains a fatal game
For show of force.
If a mighty power
Will over rule the world,
Foes will be invented
To spread fear through force.

Its vanity which is behind
The power game,
Will go on in time,
Unless history dies,
And Man is willing
To invent himself again.
Then hope may be seeded
On the road to peace.

Achilles wondered
If Priam was still awake,
Or is mumbling
Strange words in his sleep.
Whispering at him winged words
With his golden voice:

Were you speaking while sleeping,
Or musing prophecies?
Rest for tomorrow,
It's another day to weep,
Before the rosy dawn;
         You'll head with Hector home.

THE DREAM

I was having a dream
In peaceful wonderland;
An old Phoenician king,
And his subjects were drinking,
As if celebrating,
The coming of the spring,
But a blind man told me,
It's a gathering for peace.

When the Sythian mountaineers
Raided the town,
King Alimanos made them
A tempting offer
Of gold and silver,
And loads of Sidonian attires,
If they did not harm
Women and children, and the seers.

After they left in peace
Without damage or harm,
He called upon the towns people
To celebrate for life,

In drinking wine, singing
And dancing to the lyre.

As long as we have our oars
We can sail swiftly,
And ride the blue
Towards the setting of the sun,
Faster then thought,
We can replace what we have lost.
Better days of hard work
Then shedding blood and tears.

The voice of the blind man
Is still clicking in my ears
And makes me question
The real intention of this war.
If the Sythian tribesmen
Spared destruction for gold,
Then why the Achaean
Will not accept the same?

Oh Zeus these are my words,
Save us from this slaughter
And help the Achaean to reason
And end this unjust war.
Are they after Helen
Or the destruction of Troy?

Achilles was now
Entrenched in deep sleep;
Priam was awake,
Recounting his faded dreams.

If the Achaean have
A shred of wisdom,
They will think twice
Before they destroy Ilium.

Like a guarding shield,
At the tip of the hellespont,
It protect the Aegean
From barbaric raids.

It is a gate between Hellas,
And the nomads from the east,
If it is destroyed
Hellas will be raided soon.

If reason were the means
To solve human affairs,
Wars would have been prevented,
And peace would have prevailed.
But when the impulse for greed,
Over-rules the soul,
War becomes a games,
To play with peoples lives.

For rulers of tomorrow
The breed of Odysseus
Will not dismiss their gains
Nor will they blink an eye,
If they have to kill children,
And bring temples down.

Justice becomes an art
Of canny craftiness,
In order to win a battle,
Or another war.
Feeble minds with reckless temper
Often think
That wars are the golden means
To silence a foe.

They do not know
That winners on the battle field
Would become looser,
If they succumb to folly.
For this reason
Those who seek power for glory,
Often face their doom,
          Before reaching their goal.

THE RETURN

Before the full moon crossed
The mountain range,
The maidens were bathing Hector,
With laurel oil,
With mirth and mountain herb.

They cleaned his wounds.
And Achilles shrouded him
With his purple robe,
A gesture to honor
His most respected foe.

Argeiphontes mounted him
On the four wheel wagon,
And Achilles clasped Priam
On his face,
To wake him and be ready
For the long journey.

They both silently stood
Gazing eye to eye,
In this moment of grace,
Too shy for speech.

When dignity, justice and pride,
Springs from the heart,
A life time is fulfilled,
In such a blissful stand.

Firmly they shook hands,
Shoulder to shoulder clasps,
In timeless silence
When time stood still, they depart.
Glory to the spirit,
When hatred is surpassed,
And vengeance is transformed,
Into justice for all.

Priam and Idaeus,
Are now moving slowly,
Towards Ilium which soon
Will all be gone.
With anguished hearts,
Steadily they move towards Troy,
As if they wish to slide
Into forgetfulness,
Only to dream that they will come
With Hector home.

His frame still lean,
As if his soul had not left,
To protect his skin
From the Anatolian sun.

Through the rosy, misty clouds
Over the olive grove,
The carriage was breaking
The silence of the dawn,
Before it reached a stone
Throw distance from the gate,

Cassandra heard the grinding
Of her father's cart.
Quickly she rose from her
Light sleep to climb the wall,
Bursting with cries of death,
To wake the Trojans.

Oh me . . . Trojans, wake up
To welcome Hector home.
Oh me . . . Mytera,
My life without my brother
Is nothing but darkness,
Without glittering hope.

He died for his city
To save us from disgrace,
But hungry scavengers
Want more to be pleased.
Not less than our honor,
Ashes of our bones,
Our children will be slaughtered,
Women will be sold.

In the shadow of time
We will be forgotten,
No traces of our past,
No story will be told.

Ruthless Odysseus
And beastly Agamemnon
Will reduce Troy to ashes,
Before they'll be gone.

As for my brother who fought
With courage and pride,
Senseless humiliation
Was inflicted upon his corpse,
Without mercy from Zeus
Or from any rightful god.

If justice has a sword,
And truth is eternal,
Your story will resurface,
And truth will be told.

The carriage was about
To pull close to the gate,
The Trojans were lamenting Hector,
With soaring cries
As the guards were ready
To open the gate.

Andromache led the crowd,
Singing sad dirges,
Fluttering her hair,
Bursting with cries in tears,

Oh me . . . Hector, the light
From my eyes have faded;
In bleak darkness you left me
With morbid fear.

Most gentle, most kind,
Most courageous son of Troy,
The wind of fate unjustly
Took your life away;
After the fall of your shield,
All other shields will fall.
And Troy will be left
For killers to roam around.

Your son if destined to live,
Will become a slave,
And I . . . ! what master
Will I be enforced to bed,
Before he smells my roses,
I will choose to die.

Oh mother earth, why don't you
Blow away your fire
Against the Achaean ships,
And burn them down.
Oh moon, why not raise
A mighty tidal wave,
And wash the intruders
From our shores.

Oh me . . . the gods are not
Willing to see our side,
No signals from heaven
To lead us to safety.
Alone we are facing,
Our imminent doom,
And when the hour comes,
We will vanish with honor.

In spite of her old age,
Her wisdom and stoic heart,
Hecabe moved towards Hector
With swollen eyes,

Oh me . . . why the gods
Have chosen my son to die.
From your horse I saw you falling,
Like a shooting star.
Wounded at heart
From the long spear of Achilles.

Most painful pain is when
A mother loses her son,
When the heart is weak,
And the tears are dry.

I should have read more clearly
What lies ahead in time,
And given Priam better council
About the flaws of Paris.
Without probing into
The Achaean affairs,
King Agamemnon
Might not have started this war,
But what is done, is done
No time now for return,
The fall of Troy is imminent,
Quickly with your fall.

Suddenly, Helen appeared
Like a goddess in her shroud.
Descending from heaven
As if she was riding a cloud.
Wearing a mourning silky attire
Not of a Spartan custom,
But of some foreign land.

Wailing from her heart,
and her eyes soaked with tears.
Singing her own dirges,
As if she was always near.

Oh dear Hector
Most gentle of heart and soul
You were more like a brother
Through these difficult years
I know that my love to Paris
Is the cause of this war,
If I am courageous,
I should exercise a choice,
I should either have gone,
In shame and in disgrace,
Or with my own bare hand,
Taken my own life.

But my weakness at heart,
Is like Aphrodite',
When Eros strikes the soul,
Unwillingly we fall.

What a gloomy doom,
What a curse I brought to Troy.
Bringing raging fire
To this peaceful kingdom,
Because I loved Paris,
And followed my heart's call.

I left behind me the place,
Where my eyes opened to the light.
The glorious name of my Lord,
Lustrous living and fame,
And the beauty of his land.

I had no whims of my action,
Nor grasp of good or evil,
I followed the goddess' path,
Listening to my heart's call.

The love I have for Paris,
A shining light from heaven;
Most beautiful course to follow,
For peace, not for war.

But doom upon you is falling,
The crown of the Aegean.
My wish is to be buried,
    As Helen of Troy.

THE FAREWELL

Priam stepped from the cart,
Weary from his old age.
Appealing to the crowd
To clear the hall for space,
To lay Hector down
In front of Apollo's shrine.
With a prophetic voice,
Began the eulogy of Hector.

There will be no more roses,
To smell in Ilium sky,
Nor silvery olive trees
To sparkle in the sun.
The night owl will be gone,
All of us will be gone,
And there would be no reason,
To mesmerize with stories.

Troy will be ablaze
When the truce is over.
When the Achaean drench
Our land with blood and terror.

Stories will be told
Throughout the ages,
That all their warriors
With clubs and pointed spears,

Did not shake our hearts,
Nor weaken our will.
That we vanish upright,
Justly facing our doom.

Kings are born to rule
As fathers of their tribes;
With dignity for all,
Under the divine laws.
Any one's good is good
For himself and for all.

Hector fought with Valor,
Defending his city,
But lost with honor
Against mighty Achilles.
It was his choice to die,
A bliss we should revere.

The gods cannot undo
Nor lay down their control.
When mortals sweep fear away,
They become peaceful,
And Hector's death was peaceful death.
Sing for him your Trojan dirges,
But be happy for his soul
Eternity will be
          His solace and reward.

THE AFTERMATH

Before the mourning feast
For Hector was over,
And the pyre smoked
After the wine was poured.
The Achaeans ready now
For battle once again
With soaring battle cries,
To stir the blood for war,
Unleashed their horses,
To storm against the Trojans.

Achilles was like thunder,
Pounding against the guards,
When suddenly dreadful
Silence swept through the land.

Paris aimed at Achilles
From his hiding place,
And with poisoned arrow
He pinned Achilles' heel;
Faster than lightning,
The poison flowed in his veins,

Like rolling rock roaring
When tossed into the sea,
He fell from his black horse,
With blood soaking the ground.

The Achaeans were stunned,
Shattered in disbelief,
Thinking that Ilios
Smote Achilles from the clouds.

The Trojans gushed
Through the gate like a stream;
Horse riders, bare footed,
With stones, sharp knives and spears,
Tracked the Achaeans,
Like hounds after their prey.

Ajax risked his life,
To save Achilles' corpse,
And carried him away
Beyond the safety line.

The Achaeans believed,
That after Hector's death,
The war could be over,
In one damaging stroke,
But they have discovered
That the Trojan will,
Is not easily tamed
Nor broken down.

They reasoned that the war,
Could not be won in battle,
But by some unconventional means,
They could pierce the fortress' wall.

Odysseus and his peers
Made up a crafty plan,
Sending Priam a message,
Asking for peace not war.
Priam was elated,
Learning of the plan,
And sent his assurance,
For the council's safety.

They came with peaceful
Fanfare displaying games,
With a crafted replica
Of a wooden Trojan horse.
Without distrust the guards
Opened the western gate.
As soon as they toasted
Peace in cheerful mood,
The horse was opened,
And the killers swept the floor,
Flooding the hall with blood,
Like wolves in a killing field.

Ajax caught Cassandra
And raped her like a beast,
Neoptolimus thrust his sword
In Priam's heart,
And all of Troy faster than light
Was on fire.

Cassandra now was struggling
Against Ajax' hold,
With claw like fingers,
She dug into his throat;

With the tip of your sword,
Joining your comrades
To make me kneel down
For your pleasure, to the ground.

You must be
Worse than a barbarian;
In wickedness you have
No match with living beast.
What is most ignoble
Of your base qualities,
Is your conceit to think
That raping a woman,
Is an honorable deed.

I lay down upon you
My curse for endless pain.
The blood which is drawn
From me shall blind your eyes;

You will remain for ever
Deep down in Hades,
Haunted by my laughter
And scorn for your power.
For if justice did not

Punish you in this world,
Upon your conscience
I shall engrave your sin,
Where no god can help you
From torturing your own soul.

And you, Agamemnon,
Ride your vanity
Like a pitiful clown
Ignorant of your fate,
And what your end will be,
A just reward for killing
Our helpless children.

My curse shall bewilder you,
With undying shame;
Restless agonies,
And despair in your heart,
Shall spoil your glory.

And the hands of the gods
Will torture your wicked soul,
Until you give away,
The last breath of your life.

And you Odysseus,
You do not deserve to die,
Because death ends your pain,
You will wish a
Thousand times to die,
Before you reach
The gate of Hades.

On your way home,
You will be thinking
About the harvest
Of your glory,
But before you reach
The shores of your native land,
The dark turquoise Aegean
Will slam your fleet
With tidal waves,
And wash away
What you have stolen
From our temples.

And all your men, one by one,
Will vanish without mercy
To the pounding waves.
But you will survive my curse,
And the wrath of Poseidon,
For that, your image
Will be engraved in memories,
As a symbol of wickedness,
And of evil.

When blood was forced,
Foaming from Priam's throat,
Not far from choking
He spoke his last words:

When rulers willingly
Lose their sense of shame,
In dishonoring themselves
To win at any price,
It will be a sign
Of the dark days of justice.

When the breed of Odysseus
Comes to rule,
Then ruling will be
But slavery in disguise.

THE HEROES IN HADES

I am Ereshkigal,
Guardian of the underworld,
Sister of heavenly Ishtar,
Goddess of beauty and fertility.

From her throne in heaven,
She sheds her blessings
Upon our fertile land,
Sprouting the life giving crops
That nourish our people.

When our father Uranus
Struck our mother earth with lightening,
We were born twins.
Ishtar was the first
To see the rosy finger of the dawn,
And was given the seat to be
The goddess of beauty and fertility.

And I was born after the sun
Faded from the face of our land,
Was appointed to be
The guardian of the underworld,
The world of silent darkness
For restless souls.

When your fellow Cypriots
Were sailing astray
Around our shores,
Hungry and delirious,
With colorless, salty faces,
They drifted directionless
with the spiraling wind.

Ishtar appeared to them,
Wearing her shroud from heaven
And nourished them
With milk and honey
From our sacred land.

And then she gave them directions,
To set their sails westward
Towards their blissful island,
The land of love and blossoming flowers.

In moment of deep despair,
The brilliance of her aura,
Aroused their passion for life.
They re-set their sails
In the right direction,
And reached their island safely.

Upon their arrival . . .
They carved her form
From the ivory-like marble
Of their holy mountains,
As tribute to her holiness,
And sanctified her
As the goddess of their island
And gave her the name Aphrodite.

May I inform you
My most honorable guests
That you are here in this soundless,
And colorless corner of the underworld
Due to an unresolved conflict
Between your conscience and the heavenly law.
Your misfortune is that your gods
Have no sovereignty to give you assistance,
Nor do they have the power
To change the course of your fate.

If you desire to free your soul
From this eternal damnation,
You have to clean your conscience
Of your polluted judgement
In mistreating the people of troy.

It will be the most demanding task
That you have ever undertaken,
More difficult than winning
A ferocious battle against a valiant foe.

What you have to do.
Is to free your consciousness
Of your Worldly desire,
Of your EGO which has been the burden
of your lust for power and glory.

And reflect deeply upon your actions,
Taken in the past,
To reconstruct your memory
As it appears in the mirror
Of your conscience.

Your task will be only half fulfilled
When you discover
How you have polluted
Your own soul.

If I may remind you once again,
In this world of floating darkness
Egos are thrashed into ashes,
With no soothing dirges
For the young warriors
Who give their lives
On the battle-field.

And since you are now stripped
Of your worldly attire,
Of your gems,
Helmet and gears.
skinless with a faceless soul,
Therefore, you are all equal,
And will not be distinguish
Between Kings, and subjects,
Masters or slaves.

Your self purification,
Rests upon your own redemption.
You must choose eternal damnation,
Or free your soul from the chain of time
The choice is yours, and yours alone.

AGAMEMNON

What a downward spiraling turn
Reverses the cycle of my life.
What an un-ending misery
And wretched agony invades my soul.

I thought that upon my return from Troy
And before celebrating my victory
To be murdered by Clytaemestra and her sly Aegithus
Was more than I should suffer,
For what I have done to Hector's son.

But here again, I am faced
With more atrocious pain and humiliation,
As if an eternal curse,
Has fallen upon my soul,
From some unknown god.

I was born to be a ferocious king,
Not less powerful than any king
Of any time,
In conquest and glories.
I trained warriors and built
The mightiest, swiftest fleet,
And made sound treaties with powerful allies,
To fight the most stubborn foe.

I won more battles than any other king,
And displayed the best of trophies
At the shrines of Apollo,
And of the other Olympian gods.

The horses of Agamemnon
Made the earth tremble from fear,
On the battle-field,
And during peace my boundaries were secured
Against any tempted foe.

All my requests from the gods,
Were fully granted;
Even thunderous Zeus was on my side
When steaming battles were a close call.

And here I am caught in the web
Of an eternal darkness and humiliation,
As if dying once at the hands
Of my beguiling enemies were not enough
To escape from punishment in the underworld.

ACHILLES

It would have been a more peaceful world,
If we were able to have discourse
without helmets and gears.
Our restless passion for a show of force,
Blinded our minds to the truth.

Warriors in time of war
Become euphoric with
A quivering thirst for blood,
And killing for the sake of killing
Is their intoxication and their lust.
Reason becomes blinded
And peace cannot be restored.
I am the first to be guilty,
For I am zealous to kill.

In this sphere we are stripped
Of the illusion of power and glory;
Of our own self image,
Grandeur and wit, in conquering new land,
And weaving false stories.
This sphere might be the place
Where we can clear our clouded past,
Without fear that our loyalty be questioned,
Without dissention amongst our peers.

AGAMEMNON

Do I hear some doubt
About your wartime posture
As The mightiest god-like warrior,
Most courageous of all mortals,
The sharpest handler of the spear?

Son of Peleus, dearest of all the allies.
I beg you to speak freely
About what may have caused
Your doubt and grief.

As you well know, wars at times
Are necessary evils
To settle a quarrel
Or disarm a dangerous foe.
How could we have restored our honor,
Without sacking and destroying Troy?

But in reality, if Kings do not wage wars,
To subdue their enemies
And expand their empire,
Then, what are kings for?

History immortalizes those
Who were most valiant,

And those who were idle within their domain
Will be forgotten like passing clouds.
After all, if the defending forces are not used
To bring new glories
The will of the warriors may succumb to idleness,
And when for defense are needed,
They may not be ready to storm.

ACHILLES

Oh Lord Agamemnon,
You have touched upon the aching pain
Which has been brewing in my soul.
The question of a just war,
Brings me home
To my father's early schooling.

The echoes of his solemn words,
Are still alive,
Their meaning still clear,
In my mind.

Kings are like shepherds,
He told me once.
They should know how to be just,
And rule justly.

Like shepherds who use their skills
To protect their flock
From straying wolves,
Kings should have the wit and courage
To protect their people
From barbaric invasion.

Like the lions of Delos,
Who protect the treasury of the gods,
Warriors should be fearless and swift
In defending their land.

If what applies to the gods
Justly applies to man as well.
Therefore, waging a war
To defend the motherland, is a just war.

Let us not cling to our worldly feast
Of victories, and conquer again.
It will not help our cause for redemption
In this sphere.

Let the truth shed its light upon our soul
To free our consciences from guilt
And conflict with our gods.
The truth is a two edge sword my lord,
So let it fall straight forward
On my side, or against me.

ODYSSEUS

Oh Lord Agamemnon,
May I interrupt the golden speech
Of Peleus' son
To ask him why he changed
His heart and deeds.

In heated battles,
He was the most ferocious warrior;
His passion for vengeance,
Went far beyond the death of his foe.
His mighty spear can never have a swifter blow,
When pointed straight forward,
Against his mightiest foe.

And now he speaks about the truth
With some clouded,
and unknown forms
As if he were a poet,
Or a soothsayer
Of some unknown sphere.

Truth is what brings success
In wars, as well as peace.
I unashamed to use
Any kind of craftiness to win a war,
Nor any other means,
To get what I desire.

AGAMEMNON

I have not heard a word
Which stirs my curiosity,
Nor any new changes,
About your personal deeds.

You are still the same crafty Odysseus
Genius of trickery
Without ever blinking an eye,
Or having any sense of shame
To get your way at any price.
Cleverness can grant you success, but not holiness!
Since you won the race
With your tricky start
Against the swifter runner Ajax,
Until you tricked the Trojans
To enter their holy gate,
With your horse as a ploy,
I have not seen you blinking an eye,
For any misdeed you have performed,
Nor ever felt, that you have
Any sense of shame.

But when fate takes a grip,
upon your days,
You might be awakened
By the morbid call
Of your conscience,
To face your past with fear.

For now, let me go back
To the son of Peleus,
To listen to his newly
Acquired wisdom;
I may have something to learn
About how to re-cover my soul,
From my polluted past.

ACHILLES

Without any thread of doubt
In my mind.
I truly think that Odysseus
Is the most clever of the breed.

But cleverness without wisdom
And divine virtue
Can lead us astray,
And destroy harmony in our soul.
It is true that an awakening
Did take place in my heart and soul,
Which made me question
The justification of this war.

As I said before.
Truth is a two edged sword,
If we can obey its higher authority,
Without indulging in our personal affairs,
Without resuming the outer-world,
I will reveal to you
The sequence of my story.
But I must ask you,
Lord Agamemnon.
To give me your word of honor
To let the truth be revealed,
Without clinging
To our personal whims
And subjective desires.

AGAMEMNON

Go on Achilles,
Most honorable warrior of Hellas.
You are unconditionally free
To reveal what you may have surmised,
After your soul searching endeavor.

It might be a blissful moment
Which may not rise again,
To clear our conscience
From our morbid and clouded past.

ACHILLES

When I gave you my word, and honor,
To join your forces against Troy,
It was out of my conviction
That Paris' intrusion into your land,
To abduct Helen, and like a pirate,
To take away Menelaus' treasure
I was convinced that his action
Was most ignoble and provocative act.

Therefore, to bring back what is stolen
With treachery and dishonorable means,
The use of force to restore your claim.
In such a deceitful case is justified.
I had my mind and soul
With my unrilinquishing will
To fight for a noble cause.
But then events started to take
A different course.

One day you sent your heralds
With threatening order
And glossy words
To take possession
Of my beloved Briseis
As if she were your rightful prize

Since then, I lived
With restless questioning . . . .
Should I have refused
Your unjust order
And created dissention in the camp?
Or do what I have done,
Sending Briseis away
Because you are the king,
And your will is over mine.

But this stand did not resolve
My inner sense of turmoil and shame,
Because I dishonor myself
For not taking a stand,
As for dishonoring Briseis.

But this aching question
I have for you my Lord :
If you justified waging this war
Because of Paris' sinful act
In abducting Menelaus' maiden
Then how can you justify
Using threatening demands
To gain possession of my Briseis?

AGAMEMNON

Kings are law makers,
But they do not have to be
Subject to their own laws.
At times it would be a weakness,
To treat themselves as equal,
Because they could lose their power,
If they conform their will
To a sovereignty other than their own.

And in a state of war,
When passion's tide rises'
Matters of conscience
Will be over-ruled
By the whims of our subjective desire.
But when it comes to the question
As to who took the right course of action
Despite your youthful heart,
You were the wise one,
And I acted lawlessly like a barbarian tyrant,
Instead of a Hellenes
Who is bound by heavenly laws.

Now I can understand why the gods
were mocking me,
When I exhaled the last breath
Of my life, at Clytaemestra's hand.

ACHILLES

When it comes to death and dying,
My death was the most atrocious
And senseless way to die.

My heel caught a poisoned dart
Flying from Paris' hand.
The poison spread like lightning,
Swelling my heart tearing my veins
As if my whole body were on fire.

My mouth was foaming
With bitter blood,
And I was slowly losing my senses,
Like a stray dog.

How many times I wished
That I had been downed by Hectors' spear
And not instead by the most ignoble sly.
But the gods may have laid a curse upon me,
To die dishonorably
For my excessive vengeance
In abusing Hector's corpse.

I do envy Hector for his death
And the way he succumbed
With honor to the ground.
He fought straight on fiercely
Like an honorable warrior,
Shield to shield, and spear to spear,
And never did I see him blinking an eye.

I was the one who used a cunning stroke,
Which is against the warier's code of honor
To pin his thigh.
He knew too well,
That his end was coming soon
But he kept charging like a lion,
Looking at me straight in the eye.

When he departed,
He was still gazing at me,
With scorn and pity,
For winning a dishonorable fight
I never felt more drenched with shame,
In spite of winning a ferocious fight
For Patroklos' honor and pride.

AGAMEMNON

This may seem to be
A blasphemy on my part,
But the curse of Cassandra
seems to be taking its course,
Against the will of all the gods.
Because what we have done,
In battles was endorsed,
If not directed by mighty Zeus
How else can I explain
Or predicament in this sphere.

Ereshkigal, The house keeper
Of the underworld,
Reminded me of what Cassandra
Told me in her moment of rage:
"I will be eternally dwelling
In your conscience to torture you
With guilt and shame:
For what you have done to me
And to my people"

What seems to be taking course,
Is that our efforts
For self-purification
Are all in vain.

Because while her curse
Is laying down her powerful claim,
Our gods seems to be powerless
To interfere.

ACHILLES

Or else, the gods may have changed
Their tide,
Due to our excessive
Arrogance and greed.

When I was dragging Hector's corpse
Goddess Athena appeared to me
In her heavenly form,
And clasped me by my shoulders
At first sight of her presence.
I thought that she was giving me
Encouragement for performing
My acts of vengeance.
But then she appeared once again,
And gazed at me with scornful look.
As if she wanted to tell me-
It is unholy to abuse a corpse.

Was too late in realizing
What she meant that
My soul was overruled by hate
And anger for Patroklos' vengeance.

I realized, that I should regain
My senses, and stop inflicting
Senseless brutal wounds
Upon a mutilated corpse.

AJAX

That woman!
She was not born
To be tamed by any man,
Not even by almighty Zeus.
It took a three pointed spear
From the best of warriors,
To pin her down.

And yet, before I was able
To take her down,
She spat in my face
A mouthful of bitter venom,
And I felt as if waves of fire
Had blinded my eyes.

Suddenly, she collapsed
From her rage and anger
As if she were consciously
Trying to wipe these events
From her memory. .

But when she regained
Her consciousness
She looked at me fiercely,
Straight from eye to eye.

Calling me coward of all cowards,
Clown of all the clans.
Only a sly stenchy wolf,
Would do what you have done.

And then, as if transformed
Into another world,
She pointed her finger against my face,
Like a Trojan dagger,
And pronounced her unholy curse.

"May you become infertile,
Consumed with your self-hatred,
Until your bones become brittle,
And rotten like those of an old fox".

Since then I never felt
That I can have a manly posture.
I was consumed with hatred and envy,
For what other men could do.

I started to dislike my own body,
So resiliently trained
With vigor and hardship
As befitted the perfect warrior.
But now it had become a burden upon my soul.

I think the goddess Artemis,
Guardian of virgin maidens,
Finally made her stroke
To make me see illusory figures and forms.

I thought that they were my enemy,
Attacking me at dawn
Before I could be ready
With my armor and gear.

So I went on a killing frenzy,
Slaughtering everything I saw,
Until the pasture was flooded
With murky blood.

But when I was awoke
At the sound of the vultures,
I could not believe what I had done,
Nor could I bear my guilt and grief.

After I reflected upon my own inwardness,
I saw nothing but scars of shame
Menacing my soul.
I could not go on living with my self hatred,
And decided to put an end of my agonizing pain.

I pointed my sword against my heart,
And pressed downward with my own weight
Until my last breath disappeared.

ODYSSEUS

I am elated and relieved,
That you have forgotten our showdown
When I took possession of Achilles' armor and shield,
Which may have been your right to own.

AJAX

(In deep silence without answering Odysseus
But the waves of his consciousness
do speak)
You are as foxy as you can ever be,
Scoundrel at heart,
Without even attempting to hide.

You are like the chameleon
Which changes its color
To match the falling leaves,
A beguiler and with
No sense of shame.

You glaze the truth at your whim,
To serve your self deceit,
Consumed with your pitiful
Self-love and deification,
Without regard for others,
Or respect for heavenly laws.

ACHILLES

We Hellenes pride ourselves
In keeping our promises,
And honoring our word
Until it is fulfilled.

What we forget is that the truth
Is more important than our pride.
At times we may have to choose
Between the truth and our own self esteem.

But if we choose what is right
Even though it may appear
To contradict our stand,
Peace and harmony, over chaos
Will prevail.

NEOPTOLIMUS

Since we have changed our inclination,
To ponder, and to reflect upon the truth
As a way to seek repentance,
And to free our inner souls
From Bad conscience and guilt,
I should reiterate what Priam said
During his last lofty stand.
When I speared him at the edge
Of his aching heart.

I said if you tell me
Where Helen is hiding
With her treasure,
I will spare your life.

He gathered his will
And took a deep breath,
As if it was his last,
And spoke with unshaking voice
While coughing his blood:

I will be thankful if you
Free my soul from suffering
This morbid pain.

Not because life is more dear
At old age, nor for lacking the will
To perform this task.
But because it is against our norms
And principles for any man
To take his life away.

But concerning golden Helen,
As I said before,
Only her ghost may have been around.
But as a person
With her flesh and purity of form,
She never entered our gates,
Nor any fragments of Menelaus' treasure.

By then, his head was tilted downward,
Peacefully mumbling,
As if he was eulogizing Troy.
Like a stray dart
In the wind of fate,
Troy is gone,
For ever gone.

Meanwhile, Menelaus was searching
For Helen, with expectations high as the sky
And I told him what Priam said
About his golden spouse
As his last breathless words.

At first, he shrugged his shoulders,
As if he had heard a fairy tale,
Then he nearly succumbed,
In a state of disbelief.

But then he gathered his will,
And shattered hopes,
And made a call upon
The best of his men,
And set his sails
To the rising sun.

AGAMEMNON

No wonder we are all here
In this abyss with ravaging fire.
We might have been
Waging a war for a false cause.

Our gods in the outer world,
Are lovers of power
And self esteem for glory
But here, they are all meaningless.
Power it seems is an illusion
And a hindrance
To purification of our polluted souls.

Can this be the contradiction
Of man's fate?
To fight for what he thinks
Is a good cause,
Which like funneling clouds, disappears.
But now, dear Neoptolemus,
Please tell me once again
What Priam said about Menelaus' spouse,
Before my consciousness goes into sleep.

NEOPTOLIMUS

My lord Agamemnon,
His words are still clear in my mind,
As if they were still ringing in my ears.
A god-like posture with purity of form,
Can never fade away from my memory.

I shall try to repeat for you,
Priam's solemn words:
"As I said before,
The ghost of Helen
May have been roaming around,
But as a person, with her flesh
And purity of form,
She never entered our gates,
Nor any fragment
Of Menelaus treasure."

AGAMEMNON

This clearly means,
That he must have
Sent a Harold to convey this news,
In order to find peaceful means
To end the war.

ACHILLES

If you were told the truth
During the heated battle,
Would you have entertained the notion
Of changing the course of the war?

AGAMEMNON

Oh son of Peleus,
My most honorable friend,
And trusted ally:
Making this choice,
Would have been
The most difficult task
After the training of my warriors,
And the labor of gathering my allies,
Was to join my forces and to restore
The honor of the Hellenes.
How can I face them so abruptly,
To set their sails towards their home?

It would have been like the story
Of that shepherd
Who falsely sends his cry for help
To chase the wolves away from his flock.
His neighbors swiftly came to help,
But there was no wolves around.
But when the wolves did come-
And mauled his flock,
His neighbors did not make a move,
For they thought it is another lie.
With this in mind,
I would have turned a deaf ear,
Or claiming that Priam's words
Were a baffling lie.

Wars are mostly fought
For senseless reason
And if there is no threat
Of danger from a neighboring state
Kings and tyrants will invent one
In order to justify,
The use of their forces.

Warriors should be ready and swift
At any time to fight a war.
But if peaceful co-existence
Is prolonged beyond its time,
Their spirits become mellow
And their wills soon wither
And weaken from idleness,
Unfit to face an imminent danger,
Or a fierce enemy.

ACHILLES

So wars become a necessary evil,
For better or worse.
If our land is not invaded,
We have to falsify a reason
To open new frontiers.
And if we lack an enemy,
We have to create one.
Precisely for this reason
I thought that it was futile
To convey to you the news.
Besides, it would have been awkward
For me to interfere.

AGAMEMNON

Well spoken, your reasoning
As clear as can be.
I hope that I do not sound as though
Poking into your affairs,
Or a bit forward, in asking you,
If Priam made an attempt,
To negotiate for peace.

ACHILLES

One day while the sun was setting
I was still in my frenzy,
Dragging Hector with my chariot,
Around Patroklos' pyre.

The dust was nearly settled
In the battlefield,
And the waves of the war cry
Faded beyond the misty hills.

Suddenly I felt a chill
Sweeping my bones,
And my heart stopped from throbbing,
As if a mystery blinded my mind,
Unrecognized by my senses
And before I knew who was near,
Priam was solemnly standing
At the entrance of my gate,
With Argeiphontes, his best charioteer,
A guardian and a seer.

Bewildered by agony and grief,
His spirit not yet broken,
Colorless, armless, and frail,
His eyes still sparkle with dignity and self esteem.

He approached me like a defeated old lion,
Clasping on my knee, and begging,
That either spear him down
Or accept the treasure of Troy
As ransom for Hector's corpse.

An overwhelming encounter,
Beyond my senses to perceive,
And beyond my reason or understanding.
As if two men met heart to heart
In an empty desert,
Without memory of the past.

I lay my hand upon his shoulder
To give him assistance with a peaceful sign
Then, I invited him to my quarters
To spend a restful night.

During our discourse,
He granted me safety
To go freely to Troy,.
With all its doors open,
To be my own witness;
And to see with my own eyes.
If either golden Helen,
Or Menelaus treasure,
Are in between its walls.

He also begged me to give assurance,
That his offer is extended,
To you or to any council you choose,
So that peace might be restored.

After dwelling upon this matter,
I thought that the prospect
For peace were futile,
Because the war is already determined
By our forces to win the war.

But now I feel that I betrayed Priam
And my own conscience,
For peace could have come
And the truth told.

AGAMEMNON

You should not feel guilty,
Nor responsible for prolonging this war.
My mind was already anchored
In my own fixation,
A victory against the stubborn Trojan;
Otherwise I will condemn myself to live in exile,
Like a homeless beggar,
Without ever seeing Argos again.

Wars are like wild fire-balls,
Developing their own uproar;
Nothing can diminish their spiral wind,
Until they exhaust their own cause.

Regardless of what Priam's
Offer may have been,
Would not be enough to make peace,
Because it could be a demoralizing disaster
Shame would be glazing my face
If I confront my allies with this plan

ACHILLES

It seems that even if you were assured,
That neither Golden Helen,
Nor Menelaus' treasure
Are not in Troy.
The war would still go on
For a purpose of its own.

AGAMEMNON

Helen was the major cause of this war.
Fighting for dignity and pride,
Is not less important than
Winning back a piece of land.
Wars can take an unpredictable course,
Like fate, which is written
By the hands of the gods.

Regardless of unexplained reasoning,
I can either seize the moment for victory,
And a place in history will be assured;
Or yield to for wishful dreams,
Of peace and brotherhood.

ACHILLES

But what about your friends and allies
To whom you gave your word of honor
About the real cause of the war?
Can you go on enforcing your own
Subjective will
Without telling them the truth?

AGAMEMNON

During the frenzy of the battlefield,
Warriors don't think about trivial matters.
Victory is their driving force,
Not what they think to be right or wrong.

ACHILLES

But these warriors have made their vow
To fight for an honorable cause.
Would they not be cheated of their lives,
If they died in vain?

AGAMEMNON

They would have died
With honor and pride,
For being loyal to their leaders,
And for their heroic stand.

ACHILLES

What about Menelaus' journey?
Did he persuade King Proteus of Memphis
To bring Helen
And his treasure home?

AGAMEMNON

When he set his sails to the open sea,
I was already in this spiral darkness.
Therefore, I have no idea
What is happening in the outer-world.
I don't remember if he ever decided
To search for Helen in Egypt,
Or to resign himself to her bleak fate.

MENELAUS

After I heard the news from Neoptolimus,
That Helen might be stranded in Egypt,
I gathered my men, and set my sail
As swiftly as the long wing birds;
We surfed with the western breeze.

When I anchored at king Proteus' land,
To my surprise, I was given
A hearty welcome by his guards,
Who lead me to the palace of their king.

Helen was treated as a virgin maiden,
Like a priestess of the gods
Not even king Proteus
Ever approached her as his own.

And the treasure was safely stored
In a sacred temple
Where they keep the valuable gifts
For Achnaton; their divine god.

Upon my return to the open sea,
I encountered gales and whirling wind
Which made it difficult for me
To pass the delta's straight.

All that I could do was to submit
A sacrifice to merciful Poseidon.
I anchored again and picked
Two young children to submit
Their blood as libation to Poseidon,

During this span of time
An Egyptian priest,
Who possessed the power of divinity.
From their god-king,
Approached me and laid down
His eternal curse upon me
And my men,

So that we would always live.
With turmoil, guilt and pain.
They do not believe
In sacrificing human
Nor do they allow pollution
Of their land with innocent blood.

And then the priest spoke his words:
"We open the doors of our temple
With good will to safeguard your spouse,
But you came to stain our soil
With the blood of innocent children
To please your gods.
It seems that you do not have
Enough dignity to appreciate
The hospitality your spouse has been given
By our blissful king".

I will deliver you to the open sea,
Not because of our mercy toward injustice,
But because we have no place
For a sinner like you in our land.

My misfortune did not end with his curse,
But when I safely anchored in Argos
Helen deserted me to join
The Priestesses of Artemis.

I was left alone like a wandering beggar.
Living an empty life, with polluted soul.
I wished a hundred times that
My voyage to Crete had never took place
So Helen would not have been tempted
By Paris and sailed away.

AGAMEMNON

Oh goddess of the under-world,
It seems that our valiant
And most courageous heroes
Who fought for the honor of their land
Under the guidance of the Olympian gods,
Are all here caught in the web
Of eternal suffering and pain.

After we met our brutal death in the outer-world,
At the hands of our sly enemies,
Why do we have to be punished again
In being thrown into this silent darkness
Without any hopes to be free?
Is the punishment received
At the hands of our enemies,
Not enough for the wrongs we have done?

ERESHKIGAL

I am not a goddess
Nor do I have the power
To forgive or to forget.
About your outer-world sinful deeds.
I am only a care-taker
Of this silent sphere.

I can only listen to the whispers
Of your conscience
And I have no authority
To judge what I hear.

From my past experience
With prisoners of their conscience
I can only offer you advice
For what might be the right course to take;
But I cannot issue orders
Because you are the one
Who is supposed to choose.

AGAMEMNON

I beg your divinity to give me some direction
Which will lead me to the right course
Restore my freedom, and to purify my soul.

ERESHKIGAL

You seem to assume that salvation
Is easily gained,
Or can be obtained through
Means which please the gods.

May I remind you that this sphere
Is unlike the outer-world
Where you have erected temples
With pillars of marble engraved
With silver and gold
To glorify your own image through
The image of your gods.

This sphere is like a spiral darkness
Where the prisoners of their consciences
Seek to resolve the conflict
Between their consciences, and how they lived;.
But there is no god, nor judge,
To follow their rituals or laws.

Your misfortune is that you are all alone.
There is no god or prophet to guide you,
Or help you to find your path.
You may be able to lift up your soul
By reflecting upon your own misdeeds.

AGAMEMNON

We are thrown into this spiral, murky pit,
And suddenly we are told that our fate
Can only be woven with our own hands.
It is like a judge who dictates his verdict,
But offers no chance for appeal.
If this under-world is supposed to be a solace
For restless and afflicted souls with bad consciences,
Then there should be a counseling agent—
A soothsayer an oracle, or a seer.

ERESHKIGAL

But this is precisely the point; master mind of the Hellenes.
When you enjoyed the fruits of your conquest
And ruled over your new domain,
And when the dust of your mules
Quivered the heart of your enemies,
You did not take a stand to distinguish right from wrong.

But now time has come to retrieve the history of your life,
And reflect upon how you can clean your soul,
And clear your conscience of misdeed.

AGAMEMNON

I do not have any knowledge
Of how to retrieve the history of my life.
The art of reading the unknown mysteries
Of our lives, or reading future events
Belongs to the Delphic oracle
Who is nearly immortal
In possessing knowledge of the unknown.

ERESHKIGAL

Retrieving the history of your life
Is restoring memory of your past.
No oracle, even an immortal god,
Can read the hidden events under
The layers of your conscience.

Some events may be shameful,
Or excessively painful for what
You may have done to yourself or others.
In order to escape self confrontation
Consciousness can be allusive,
Hiding what is not pleasant
By forgetfulness.
But this cunning is only an escape from the truth,
It will not help recovering the soul from bad conscience.

ACHILLES

I may have a hint of what it means
To retrieve the history of ones life
In order to have a grasp of our past
Actions and deeds.
A long time ago after I had
My encounter with Priam
A new revelation about life and death appeared.

In spite of being disintegrated
And about to lose the war,
He was self contained,
In harmonious balance
And With inner peace,
As if he expected what is imminent
Without anguish or fear.

Despite of being victorious,
Whose soul was over-ruled by passion,
Blinded by hubris and self deceit
His presence caused a lightning
Awakening of soul from deep slumber,
As if I had been conversing with sage
From far away places,
A spiritual mentor,
Or a prophet-like seer.

Since then, I have questioned my being
As well as my doing-
In taming wild horses,
Wrestling with lions,
Spearing the seven headed hydra,
Proving that I was superior
To all other mortals in strength
And in the art of war.

Having this prophecy on my shoulders,
And thus destined for the most meaningless death
In the prime of my years,
I dismissed the call,
Because I was blinded by passion,
Disregarding death which could be near.

What was revealed to me from Priam's presence
Was asking whose life
Was ending with an atrocious disaster
And not allowing the fear of death
To disrupt his harmony and peace.
A thought passed by my mind like a phantasm,
As we prepare ourselves to live for conquest,
We should also prepare ourselves to die.

ERESHKIGAL

When one is living in the outer world
This is the rightful path to follow.
Preparing oneself to die
Is the highest of all virtues.

Highest, because when a person
Comprehends in a moment of reflection
His life span, and find only meaningless
Traces of his shadowy past
And faded echoes in memory.
And then when he tries to transcend
His presence into timelessness
And find nothing; most morbid emptiness.

This fear of nothingness
Forces man to leap beyond his reasoning,
And idealize a being as god-like savior
To sooth his tormented soul
When facing the void.

But he does not realize
That if his becoming ends with nothingness,
A bliss of heavenly peace
Will embrace his soul.
While losing his ego-centric consciousness,
His consciousness will become part of the whole.

AGAMEMNON

It sounds as if our agonies
Do not have an end in sight.
Here we are in the labyrinth of miseries,
Trying to purify conscience
In order to free the soul.

But now, heavenly care taker of this world,
You are conveying mixed messages
Shattering our hope,
And clouding our minds with deep despair.

After all, if our end is nothingness
Why should we not accept our fate
As prisoners of this darkness
Without meaningless efforts
To free the soul.

ERESHKIGAL

Oh master mind Agamemnon . . .
I think that you are unwilling to forget
Your glorious past,
And the charm of power
In sacking and destroying Troy.

But here in this under-world, the world of silence
Your victories are meaningless,
And your power is not only an illusion,
But an impediment to resolving your conflict
Between your desire for power,
And liberation of your soul.

What I suggest for you
Is to reflect upon what helps you to have
A soundless, peaceful sleep.
Planing to wage war for new conquest,
Or implementing good deeds
In order to make a better world.

ACHILLES

This reminds me what my father used to say,
When he used to gave me some schooling
During my growing years:
"Wisdom has taught me that a just ruler
Is the one who tries to make the world better,
Instead driving for power and glories,
And remember that it takes years to build
A shrine for the goddess of justice,
But only foolish moments to destroy."

Another event which is nearly forgotten,
Should have made a stronger
Impression upon my life;
But the foolishness of a youthful heart
Did not help me to grasp its meaning at that time.

I was on my hunting trail,
And about to spear a long horn boar.
Suddenly, an old mule shattered
The break of dawn with his bray
And left me too un-focused
And perplexed to pull my bow.

Here an old man with a frail frame
And wobbling knees guided his mule
Through the rocky path
To reach his olive grove
At the foot of the mountain.

I approached him with wonder and humble respect
And asked: "where are you heading
Through this rocky path
Which is difficult even for the young to follow?"

He raised his head like an old grey eagle,
With piercing eyes and cracking cough
In between the rhythm of his well chosen words:
"Nothing is difficult enough
To do what I suppose to do
Which is tending my daily tasks:
"I tended these tender olive trees from seed,
To plant them before I leave
At my children's olive grove."

"But my dear sir,
You are too old to perform this difficult task.
Why don't you get some help from your children?"
"Nothing would be more pleasing he said,
Than to plant a dream for the coming of time.
Besides, what could be more of a bliss
Than to be a part of the cycle of life?
As I have harvested what my father,
And grand father planted,
So I am planting for my grand children."

AGAMEMNON

Oh warrior of all time,
I never thought of you
As a good story teller.
But this one sounds like a parable
Cited in a holy scripture
From the east.

But what is astonishing to me
Is your persistent change of heart
Which begins to take hold of me,
Which makes me feel perplexed,
And question the way we waged war.
How many wheat fields
And olive groves we set on fire,
In order to starve our enemies
And force them to surrender.

Your story about the old man
Made me realize
How much pain we inflicted
Upon human hearts,

How much suffering we inflicted
Upon innocent women and children
In destroying their cities
And dislocating their homes.

But alas war is war,
Sometimes a necessary evil:
But it may be that when
Evil forces consume each other,
The GOOD may be rooted again

ERESHKIGAL

A change of heart is the miracle of miracles
Which no immortal god can perform.
Man is his own savior,
And if he chooses the path of salvation
There is no Pithia nor soothsayer
To shed light upon the darkness,
To free his soul from its own self torture
Due to his bad conscience
For polluting the outer-world.

Achilles' words cannot be better said:
"what is needed is to undergo self purification,
A task which is more difficult than waging war,
But not impossible to reach"

What all of you might realize is
That all the shrines you have constructed
In order to be remembered,
All the temples you designed
To glorify your own image,
And the glorification of
Your anthropomorphic gods,

All the towers you have raised
To follow the movement of the heavenly bodies:
In time, all will crumble into ashes
Like dust in the wind;

All the wars which you have fought
With valor and Hellenic pride,
All the gold and silver
You have gathered
From sacking cities
And conquering new lands,
All will fade away like an echo of a whisper
In fading memories.

You have left behind,
Only those peaceful moments
Of your soul,
What you have done with good conscience
To serve your people.
And when time elapses
In your consciousness into timelessness,
You will realize how meaningless
Your striving for power appears.

ACHILLES

I never felt more at ease
To be evolving into imagelessness,
As if the burden to live up to my image,
Was my enslavement, but now I feel
As if my soul were released into endless freedom.

AGAMEMNON

It was not only my lust for power and conquest
Which made me lead a restless life,
But also my blind passion for rivalry,
And to win the woman I desired at any price.
What a good feeling to be free from manly desires
And illusory needs like a smokeless fire
Which comes into being and fades away
Without leaving any traces in memory.

If I had a seed of wisdom in my mind.
I would have had a more peaceful life.
And led my people to a state of well-being,
And prosperous life, instead of wars.

ERESHKIGAL

It is a pity, that after you left the outer-world,
And entered the gate of hades you were awakened,
As if the glow of a heavenly light,
Enlightened your consciousness
To make you see through
The mirror of you conscience
The images of your life story.
From all the signs that I decipher
You are amongst the lucky ones.
Your soul might be liberated
From the burden of your ego,
The cause of your destructive volition
And self-glorification

Time is the judge . . .
That your soul may become free to sail
Into timeless nothingness.
The wonder of wonders:

If your fellow men
In the outer-world,
Will ever allow reason to prevail
In resolving conflicts
Instead of waging wars,
They will learn in their life times
What you have learned after your death.

In every-dayness
Man is walking toward death.
As he work hard to meet his daily needs,
He should also be prepared
To confront his final days,
With good conscience peacefully.
It is the only path for salvation,
Simplest of all endeavor,
Yet most difficult to follow.

A note about this poem

At old age, we reflect upon our life to assess what we have done, and what we used to dream about doing. However, while some dreams were actualized others remained alive but only as sheer phantasm in our memory. Since my youthful years, when I first read the Iliad, the images of ACHILLES dragging the corpse of Hector never faded from my memory. Unnecessary ruthlessness for revenge and hatred were unleashed without control. The images of this poem have been in a state of hibernation in my mind for a very long time, compulsively few summers ago, I found myself sketching them into words.

I.S

BVG